O star of wonder, star of light,
Star with royal beauty bright,
Westward leading, still proceeding,
Guide us to thy perfect light.

JOHN H. HOPKINS, JR.

STAR OF

Wonder

STAR OF WONDER

When they had heard the king,
they departed; and, lo, the star,
which they saw in the east, went before them,
till it came and stood over
where the young child was.
When they saw the star, they rejoiced
with exceeding great joy.

MATTHEW 2:9–10 KJV

*A*nd suddenly there was with the angel
a multitude of the heavenly host praising God,
and saying, Glory to God in the highest,
and on earth peace, good will toward men.

LUKE 2:13–14 KJV

STAR OF

Wonder

In the hectic flurry of holiday activities, the angel's message can easily be lost. In an effort to celebrate to the fullest, we sometimes place unrealistic demands on ourselves. When the season comes to an end, we may realize we have not celebrated peace, but rather buried it beneath a mountain of obligations. During this season of peace and goodwill, may we remember the news proclaimed so joyously on that night centuries ago: "Glory to God in the highest, and on earth peace, good will toward men."

I heard the bells on Christmas day
Their old familiar carols play,
And wild and sweet
The words repeat
Of peace on earth, goodwill to men!

And in despair I bowed my head;
"There is no peace on earth," I said;
"For hate is strong
And mocks the song
Of peace on earth, goodwill to men!"

Then pealed the bells more loud and deep,
"God is not dead; nor doth He sleep!
The wrong shall fail,
The right prevail,
With peace on earth, goodwill to men!"

HENRY WADSWORTH LONGFELLOW

STAR OF

PEACE IS LIKE. . .

- a gentle dove arriving on quiet wing with its soothing message.
- a bubbling brook which flows unmindful over the obstacles in its path.
- a soft breeze that caresses and refreshes our spirit.

*M*ary must have suffered some anxiety as she awaited the birth of her son. Joseph, too, may have wondered what the future held for his family. But the star that came to rest over the place where the Christ child lay brought a message of its own. It led visitors to Bethlehem—visitors who worshiped the babe. Surely this confirmation brought peace to Mary and Joseph that this was a holy night, and the child was indeed, the Prince of Peace.

STAR OF

Wonder

STAR OF WONDER

*S*ilent night! Holy night!
All is calm, All is bright,
Round yon Virgin, Mother and Child,
Holy Infant, so tender and mild,
Sleep in heavenly peace,
Sleep in heavenly peace.

JOSEF MOHR

"My soul magnifies the Lord, and my spirit
has rejoiced in God my Savior."

LUKE 1:46–47 NKJV

*M*ay you have the gladness of
Christmas which is hope;
the spirit of Christmas which is peace;
the heart of Christmas which is love.

AVA V. HENDRICKS

STAR OF

Wonder

Wonder

When my heart is at peace,
the world is at peace.

CHINESE PROVERB

Where there is faith, there is love;
Where there is love, there is peace;
Where there is peace, there is God;
And where there is God; there is no need.

LEO TOLSTOY

There is but one way
to tranquility of mind and happiness,
and that is to account
no external things thine own,
but to commit all to God.

EPICTETUS

While looking through a box of old holiday photos, I studied the facial expressions of friends and family. In one picture, three ladies sat on the floor, one smiling; one solemn; the other with her eyes closed against the flash. The camera captured yawning faces, surprised faces, and even a few tired faces. But the overriding expression on young and old alike was peace. I noticed how we had changed as we grew older; hairlines had receded, weight fluctuated, and gray strands of hair replaced dark ones, but still we exhibited peace. It came into each of our lives through Christ. The same peace still exists for those who seek it.

It came upon the midnight clear,
That glorious song of old.
From angels bending near the earth
To touch their harps of gold!
"Peace on the earth, good will to men,
From heaven's all gracious King!"
The world in solemn stillness lay
To hear the angels sing.

EDMUND H. SEARS

STAR OF

Wonder

Wonder

Imagine the joy of the Father
as He looked at His newborn Son.
It must have lit all of heaven with praise
to see what the Heavenly Father had done.
The angels joined their voices
with the heavenly throng,
Until their laughter filled the
air with joy and jubilant song!
And those on earth in one small realm could
only guess the joy
As Mary and Joseph held the hand of God's
redeeming boy.
We too can join the celestial chorus that began
so long ago
As we embrace the Father's Son sent from
heaven to earth below.

PAMELA F. DOWD

"You will go out in joy and be led forth
in peace."

ISAIAH 55:12 NIV

These things I have spoken unto you,
that in me ye might have peace.
In the world ye shall have tribulation:
but be of good cheer;
I have overcome the world.

JOHN 16:33 KJV

STAR OF WONDER

How comforting to serve a God who wants to give us peace. His Word assures that He speaks to us for that reason. Even though we may have problems, He encourages us to be of good cheer. He is the bearer of good tidings, bringing us comfort and joy.

*G*od rest you merry, gentlemen,

Let nothing you dismay,

Remember Christ our Savior

Was born on Christmas Day,

To save us all from Satan's power

When we were gone astray:

O tidings of comfort and joy,

comfort and joy,

O tidings of comfort and joy.

TRADITIONAL ENGLISH CAROL

Wonder

STAR OF

God's peace can come at any time. It's not limited to good times or calendar days. No watch controls it; no man can change it; no enemy can take it from you. You can experience God's magnificent gift of peace at anytime during the year. But what better time to receive this gift than during the season of peace on earth, goodwill to men.

PEACE IS. . .

- gazing at the stars with the knowledge that you know their Creator.
- closing your eyes in sleep without fear of tomorrow.
- the stillness in your heart when trouble swirls around you.
- a quiet mind in a raging world.

Wonder

STAR OF

STAR OF Wonder

For unto us a child is born, unto us a son
is given: and the government shall be upon his
shoulder: and his name shall be called
Wonderful, Counsellor, The mighty God,
The everlasting Father, The Prince of Peace.

ISAIAH 9:6 KJV

A CHRISTMAS PRAYER FOR YOU

*M*ay the peace of the Christ child
fill your mind and spirit, shutting out the
frustration and anxiety brought on by a world
in turmoil. May you have the mind of Christ
as you celebrate His birth.

STAR OF

Wonder

STAR OF WONDER

*A*nd the peace of God, which passeth
all understanding, shall keep your hearts and
minds through Christ Jesus.

PHILIPPIANS 4:7 KJV

God sent a star to light the night for The Way, The Truth, The Life—His Son. He sent the Light of Life to prove His heart so we would invite His Son into our own. God has given us all the light we'll ever need to find peace on earth, goodwill to men.

Pamela F. Dowd

"I am the light of the world.
He who follows Me shall not walk in darkness,
but have the light of life."

John 8:12 NKJV

Star of Wonder

THE PEACE OF CHRISTMAS IS NOT...

- presents piled under a decorated tree.
- a table loaded with food.
- a charge card pushed to the limit.
- the company party.
- more lights than anyone else in the neighborhood.
- giving a more expensive gift.

THE PEACE OF CHRISTMAS IS. . .

- hearing again the story of Christ's birth.
- singing age-old carols you believe in.
- watching children perform the nativity story.
- being in the company of those you love.
- realizing that all the trappings are nice, but not necessary.
- knowing the Christ of Christmas is reality.

STAR OF Wonder

VOICES IN THE MIST

The time draws near the birth of Christ.
The moon is hid, the night is still.
The Christmas bells from hill to hill
Answer each other in the mist.

Four voices of four hamlets round,
From far and near, on mead and moor,
Swell out and fail, as if a door
Were shut before me and the sound:

Each voice four changes on the wind,
That now dilate, and note decrease,
Peace and goodwill, goodwill and peace,
Peace and goodwill, to all mankind.

—ALFRED TENNYSON

Great peace have they
which love thy law:
and nothing shall offend them.

PSALM 119:165 KJV

*B*lessed are the peacemakers:
for they shall be called
the children of God.

MATTHEW 5:9 KJV

Wonder

For Christ is born of Mary,
And gathered all above,
While mortals sleep, the angels keep
Their watch of wondering love.
O morning stars, together
Proclaim the holy birth!
And praises sing to God the King,
And peace to men on earth.

PHILLIPS BROOKS